SPIES
CODEBREAKERS
Lost Words

CAREY SCOTT

ticktock

Copyright © ticktock Entertainment Ltd 2009
First published in Great Britain in 2009 by ticktock Media Ltd.,
The Old Sawmill, 103 Goods Station Road, Tunbridge Wells, Kent, TN1 2DP
ISBN 978 1 84696 899 0 pbk
Printed in China

CONTENTS

INTRODUCTION 4-7

Chapter 1 WORLD WAR II Secret Agents 8-15

Chapter 2 WORLD WAR II Secret Messages 16-23

Chapter 3 THE COLD WAR Soviet and US spies 24-31

Chapter 4 POPULAR CULTURE Spy Stories 32-35

Chapter 5 LATEST DEVELOPMENTS Espionage Now 36-39

Chapter 6 MAJOR FIGURES People in Espionage 40-43

GLOSSARY 44-45

INDEX 46-47

ACKNOWLEDGMENTS 48

INTRODUCTION

Spies and codebreakers have been around as long as there have been secrets to steal and codes to crack. Almost every government in the world uses, or has used, espionage to find out what other countries are up to. In the last 70 years or so, spies and codebreakers have helped shape the modern age. Both espionage and breaking secret codes helped win World War II. Espionage was also the most important weapon of the Cold War. Over that time period and through the present, the ways that spies and codebreakers work has changed dramatically as technological know-how has increased.

Most espionage is conducted by intelligence agencies. These are government organisations that use spies to collect secret information. Governments use intelligence agencies to find things out about foreign countries that they could not otherwise discover. They may also use these agencies to spy on people in their own countries. Most countries have one organisation for gathering intelligence at home (in Britain MI5, in the United States the FBI) and another for working abroad (MI6 and CIA respectively). Both kinds of organisation also carry out counterintelligence – protecting against enemy espionage. Most governments use espionage in peacetime as well as in war, and some conduct it against friendly nations as well as hostile ones. Intelligence gained from 'friendly' and peacetime spying can give advantages at the negotiating table and in business. In wartime, espionage is used most often to try to gain a military advantage.

MILITARY SECRETS
Military secrets could be technical information about the development of new weapons, troop movements, or the locations of weapons

Above Spies have always used gadgets to help them carry out espionage. This watch with a hidden camera was made in 1886.

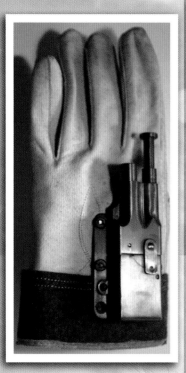

Above This glove-pistol issued by the US Navy during World War II gave a spy the advantage of being armed while keeping both hands free. To fire the pistol, one needed only to push the plunger into an attacker's body.

factories. In wartime, knowing where the enemy's troops are going can give a massive advantage, but military secrets are important in peacetime, too. During the Cold War, both the United States and the Soviet Union were anxious to know the number and size of the other's nuclear weapons. Each side felt that this knowledge gave it an advantage in the event of a real war.

POLITICAL SECRETS

Political secrets can give the spying government massive advantages in international relations. If a government knows what kinds of political or trade alliances or treaties a nation is working on with other nations, that government can plan its own strategy and form its own alliances.

ECONOMIC SECRETS

Economic secrets are those that are most commonly targeted today. These might give technical information about new inventions or other developments that are worth lots of money. New advances in communications technology, for example, or advances in genetics, can be very valuable. Being able to copy another country's technology can help to make a country rich. If a new invention has a military use it can be used to benefit another country's security as well.

WHO THEY ARE

A professional spy, sometimes called an intelligence officer or an agent, is a highly trained member of an intelligence agency. He or she may work openly in a friendly country. In an unfriendly country, the spy would probably work covertly – under cover of a false occupation, usually as a diplomatic staff member. Intelligence officers both gather information themselves, and employ non-professional spies. In this role they are sometimes called handlers. Non-professional spies are likely to be people whose jobs give them access to secret information. These spies, either for money or because of their beliefs, then pass that information to a foreign government via their handler. An effective intelligence officer may have a whole network of such spies passing them information.

Above *Satellite dishes can be used to intercept email and phone communication. Some people argue that there is too much surveillance in modern societies.*

Above *A map of occupied territory, cleverly secreted inside an ordinary playing card, was used by British spies during World War II.*

Left *Front view of the MI6 building in London.*

A WORLD OF TAPS AND BUGS

The traditional way that spies collect their information is by recording private conversations and copying secret documents. Cold War spies used miniature cameras, some so tiny that they were disguised as coat buttons, to photograph documents. Telephone taps and 'bugs' (tiny, concealed microphones) were widely used and, in the 1960s, KGB (Soviet secret service) officers even bribed hotel staff to plant bugs inside the heels of the shoes of visiting Western diplomats.

Above *The Watergate Hotel, scene of the break-in and wire-tapping scandal that eventually led to the resignation of US president, Richard Nixon in 1974.*

A miniature transmitter, microphone, and batteries made the target a walking radio station, transmitting conversations to a nearby monitoring post.

CODES AND CIPHERS

The business of stealing secrets also involves sending, intercepting, and interpreting messages. Before the twentieth century, individuals created codes and ciphers for sending secret messages for a number of different reasons. Individual codebreakers cracked, or solved, the codes and ciphers, too. This changed around 1917, when the first cipher machine was invented. This machine automatically 'encrypted' the text typed on its keyboard, converting the 'plain' text into 'code' or 'cipher' text. In the language of codebreaking, these types of text are often known as 'plaintext', 'codetext', and 'ciphertext'. The recipients of the message set their machine up in the same way as the sender's to convert the message back to plaintext.

By 1939, when World War II broke out, the military on both sides was using cipher machines to encrypt their messages. The governments of the warring nations urgently wanted to read each other's messages to find out their military plans. But it proved impossible for individual codebreakers to crack these new ciphers. In Britain and the United States, teams of very talented matheticians were gathered together, and they were able to build machines that could carry out the millions of calculations needed to read the messages. The machines that they built were the forerunners of modern computers. Today, people with coding skills work in computer technology, as programmers – codemakers –

Above *This ballpoint pen has been stripped away to show the tiny radio transmitter built inside it.*

or illegally as hackers – codebreakers. The use of computers to store information and the invention of the Internet has changed the role of the spy as well as the codebreaker. Often, spies can access quite valuable information on the Internet, or, if they have the codebreaking skills, can hack into protected computer networks to steal or access secret information.

DIGITAL SPYING

Digital technology has enabled the modern spy to steal information more easily and more effectively than ever before. The modern spy can choose from a huge range of digital spying tools disguised as everyday objects. In some cases, the technology has even taken over altogether. 'Spies in space' satellites hover above our planet, observing events in such detail they can even record and transmit the headline on a newspaper, and 'ears in space' satellites capture telephone and computer data and relay it to ground stations for analysis.

Above *Spy satellites are valuable tools for military intelligence gathering. As they orbit the Earth, they photograph different countries' military installations.*

These are huge advances since the earliest days of those military satellites launched in the 1960s. The first of these were known as the KeyHole series, and faced the challenge of retrieving the film from the cameras within the satellite. The operators ejected the (undeveloped) film towards Earth, within a container. When the container entered the upper atmosphere, a parachute deployed which slowed its progress. The film package was then caught in mid-air by an airplane sent to its expected point of entry. This astonishingly difficult feat was remarkably successful, accomplished most of the time, and continued to be used until 1972.

Below *Between February 2001 and March 2002 British hacker Gary McKinnon used a dial-up modem and commonly available software to hack into dozens of US Army, Navy, Air Force, and Department of Defense computers, as well as 16 NASA computers. He claims to have been looking for information on UFOs, and meant no harm. If convicted, he could face up to 70 years in prison.*

Left *Matt Damon plays ex-CIA operative Jason Bourne in the film* The Bourne Identity. *Films like this and the* Mission: Impossible *series have helped to create an image of modern spies.*

WORLD WAR II SECRET AGENTS

Above *These false identity papers were made for British SOE agent Nancy Wake to enable her to operate in France during World War II.*

World War II was a global conflict in which most of the world's nations were allied to one or the other side. The opponents were known collectively as the Allies, chiefly led by Britain, the United States and the Soviet Union, and the Axis, led by Germany, Japan and Italy. As the armies of these nations fought each other, a secret or 'shadow' war was being fought alongside them.

The soldiers of this shadow war were agents, or spies, and double agents – spies who decided or were persuaded to change from one side to the other. Agents gathered information and supported the resistance fighters – citizens who fought their own war, much of it clothed in secrecy, against enemy forces occupying their homeland. Double agents were able to obtain the enemy's military secrets and to spread misinformation – incorrect information designed to mislead the enemy.

SCHOOLS FOR SPIES

In 1940, British prime minister Winston Churchill established an organisation to recruit and train secret agents and transport them to enemy territory. It was called the Special Operations Executive (SOE). Two years later a similar organisation, the Office of Strategic Services (OSS), was established in the United States. By 1944, these two organisations controlled a secret army of more than 20,000 spies. Unlike the military, this shadow army was made up

Right *Joseph Stalin, Franklin D. Roosevelt and Winston Churchill at the Teheran Conference, Persia, World War II.*

"We must use many different methods, including military sabotage, labour agitations and strikes, continuous propaganda, terrorist acts against traitors and German leaders, boycotts and riots."

Hugh Dalton, the first boss of the SOE, which trained British spies during World War II, on tactics for fighting the shadow war.

of an unconventional group of individuals. Prospective spies had to be familiar with an occupied country and fluent in its language. In addition to those qualities, nerves of steel and quick wittedness were the main credentials. People from all backgrounds and areas of civilian life were admitted: a professional wrestler, a would-be poet, a former baseball star, even convicted criminals. Female spies included a circus acrobat and a princess from India.

At SOE training schools in Britain and a 'university of espionage' called Camp X in Canada, spy trainees learned the techniques of guerrilla warfare – a type of combat that takes place in settings that are familiar to local fighters, but difficult for conventional armies to get around in, such as forest, city, or mountain terrains. Candidates were taught how to kill silently, trained to use ciphers and Morse code, and shown methods of sabotage. At Camp X students underwent a series of rigorous tests to find out if they could think on their feet, ending in 'real' missions, such as planting fake explosives on a railway. If they were caught the OSS would not help them. As part of his training, one student was interrogated and beaten by the FBI, but he still did not reveal his identity. At the end of the course, the new recruits were invited to a party. But even that was a test – to see if they would reveal their cover stories under the influence of alcohol.

Above *Resistance saboteurs from both Europe and the United States used demolition charges like this to set off explosions. The item on the left is the firing device.*

TIMELINE
1918-1939

1918
Enigma cipher machine is patented by a German businessman who sells it to banks and businesses.

1920
William Friedman coins term 'cryptanalysis'.

FEBRUARY 1926
Enigma machine is bought by the German navy to make their communications secure.

MAY 1929
Signals Intelligence Service (SIS) established as codebreakers for US Army and headed by William Friedman.

DECEMBER 1932
Team of mathematicians at the Polish Cipher Bureau solves the Enigma code for the first time.

JULY 1939
Poland gives British Intelligence valuable material on Enigma.

"What they teach you at sabotage school will blow your mind. Six or seven people that are properly trained can cripple a good-sized city. It is as easy as can be . . . . We learned how to operate and destroy locomotives and power plants, communications systems, and telephones. We also learned how to make people sick by poisoning a city's water supply . . . . . [S]tuff like that — we were taught how to fight dirty."

Frank Gleason, former wrestler and OSS recruit.

Below *As a spy for the United States, Fritz Kolbe passed on important information about military developments in the Axis countries.*

THE RIGHT EQUIPMENT

Once they had 'graduated', agents were supplied with everything they needed to operate as spies in an enemy country. Expertly forged passports, identity and ration cards, driving licences, and work permits were all provided. Axis counterespionage experts could tell from how a suit was tailored that it was made in Britain or the United States, so local clothing was obtained where possible. Dental work was even redone to look as though a local dentist had carried it out.

Agents needed to be able to defend themselves as well as to fit in, and they were equipped with specially designed weapons worthy of James Bond, such as the 'Stinger', a tiny gun disguised as a pen, or a deadly blade inside the heel of a shoe. Commonly, one coat button was actually a suicide pill. A number of captured agents did indeed bite down on these deadly buttons to avoid interrogation.

ESPIONAGE SUCCESSES

SOE spies, working for Britain, operated in all the countries occupied by Nazi Germany, but the biggest group was in France, where the resistance movement was strongest. While the SOE was mostly concerned with supporting the resistance with direct action, such as acts of sabotage, OSS agents working for the United States were more concerned with intelligence gathering. The US organisation had its biggest success in Switzerland, where future CIA leader Allen Dulles recruited one of the most successful spies of the war. In 1942 Dulles was assigned to Berne, Switzerland, as head of a small team of OSS officers to gather intelligence about the enemy. Switzerland was a neutral country but it was surrounded by the Axis, making it an ideal – if somewhat dangerous – base for spying on the enemy. In Berne, a German diplomat called Fritz Kolbe offered to spy for the British, but they suspected him of being a double agent and turned him down. Kolbe then approached Dulles, who had him and his background vetted, or checked, by counterintelligence before taking him on.

It soon became clear that Dulles had made the right decision. Kolbe was motivated purely by a hatred of Nazism, refused any payment,

1. You have been given a cover story and papers in the name of Yves Le Bras, which you will use for your normal life in the field. To cover your personality as an agent you will use the name BASTIEN.

2. You will receive and send messages for Elie's circuit. You will send only those messages which are passed to you by Elie or which are approved by him. . . . The circuit password of Elie and Paul is:

'Je viens de la part de Celestin.'

'Ah, oui, le marchand de vin.'

'I come on behalf of Celestin. Ah, yes, the wine-merchant.'

COMMUNICATION

1. You will sever your contact with the people who receive you as soon as possible and, after that, will refrain from contacting members of any circuit apart from your own.

2. As regards your wireless communication with us, we would stress that you should only be on the air when necessary and that your transmissions should be as short as possible.

Part of a typical set of orders for an SOE spy about to enter German-occupied France.

Right *Testing the V2 rocket in New Mexico, in the late 1940s. V2s were fired at cities in Britain and other European nations during World War II.*

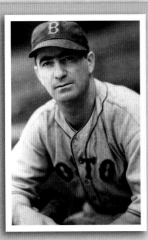

Following his 15-year career with five different major league teams, the Princeton-educated Berg served as a highly successful Office of Strategic Services (OSS) operative during World War II. Among his many missions on behalf of OSS, the former catcher was charged with learning all he could about Hitler's nuclear bomb project.

Because of his intellect, Moe Berg is considered the "brainiest" man ever to have played the game. He spoke a dozen languages fluently and often autographed pictures in Japanese.

Taken from a placard in a display case at the CIA Exhibit Center in Langley, Virginia, honouring Moe Berg. A former Major League catcher, Berg was an espionage agent during World War II.

and often put himself at great risk to obtain information. Moreover, his intelligence was of the highest quality. Over the next two years, Kolbe passed more than 2,000 documents detailing Nazi secrets to Dulles. One of the problems facing Dulles was how to transport the material – in the form of maps, drawings and reports – out of Switzerland through enemy territory to the OSS headquarters in the city of Algiers, in North Africa. He devised a complicated courier system that took 10-12 days. In Berne, the documents were photographed onto microfilm, and the film was given to the driver of a train headed for Lyon, France. The driver hid the film in a secret compartment near the engine.

On arrival in Lyon the driver passed it to an OSS agent, who bicycled it to Marseille, in the south of France. From there it was transported to the French island of Corsica by ship, and then to Algiers by plane. It was never intercepted and Kolbe was never discovered. His intelligence warned the Allies that a German agent was working in the British ambassador's home in Turkey. He also reported on the development of the V1 and V2 rockets which would rain down on London in the last days of the war, and described Japanese military plans in Southeast Asia.

OPERATION DOUBLE CROSS

Back in Britain at the start of the war, the intelligence agency MI5 was dreaming up a scheme called Operation Double Cross. In 1939, Germany began parachuting spies into Britain in an attempt to gather intelligence for the invasion they were planning ('Operation Sealion' which was never put into action). In contrast with British spies placed in enemy territory, most German agents were woefully unprepared for the adventure ahead. They had little

TIMELINE 1939-1940

SUMMER 1939
Bletchley Park becomes the British centre for intelligence interception, decryption, and distribution of German messages.

SEPTEMBER 1939
Britain and France declare war on Nazi Germany after Poland is invaded.

Above *German troops march into Poland.*

1940
The Twenty Committee begins running Operation Double Cross in Britain.

MARCH 1940
Alan Turing produces the first Bombe, an Enigma decoding machine.

JULY 1940
Special Operations Executive (SOE) established by Winston Churchill in Britain to conduct an underground war.

"My aim was to help shorten the war for my unfortunate countrymen and to help concentration camp inmates avoid further suffering."

✉ **Fritz Kolbe, in a letter written from his home in Switzerland in 1965.**

GERMANY FINALLY HONOURS THE 'TRAITOR' SPY WHO GAVE NAZI SECRETS TO AMERICA

Kolbe was described by the CIA as the most important spy of the Second World War. As a bureaucrat in Adolf Hitler's foreign ministry, he smuggled 2,600 secret Nazi documents to American intelligence in Switzerland from 1943 onwards, continuing his task undetected until the war ended. . . . Yet after the war, Kolbe was dismissed as a traitor by successive German governments. His attempts to rejoin the foreign ministry were repeatedly rejected and he was forced to end his days working as a salesman for an American chainsaw company, until his death in Switzerland in 1971.

Extract from an article in The Independent newspaper, 25 September, 2004.

Right *Thousands of these folding motorcycles, called Welbikes, were parachuted into occupied Europe for use by British SOE agents.*

Above *Allied air force planes drop supplies to agents waiting on the ground in occupied Holland.*

training, spoke poor English, and their documents were clumsily forged. Most were easily spotted, and others gave themselves up. In all, 138 German agents landed on Britain's shores, and each one ended up in the hands of MI5. Some were executed, some imprisoned, but 40 of them were persuaded to become double agents for Operation Double Cross. They began transmitting back to Germany false intelligence – a carefully calculated mixture of real but unimportant facts and misinformation devised by the Double Cross Committee. The Nazis were convinced, and MI5 was able to mislead the German Intelligence organisation – the Abwehr – for the rest of the war.

THE MAKING OF A SUPERSPY

The Double Cross Committee groomed one of its agents, Danish-born Wulf Schmidt (codename Tate), as a 'superspy'. They created a mythical network of spies for Tate. This gave the appearance that he was able to collect intelligence on many topics, encouraging his Nazi handlers to ask more questions to which false answers could be given.

Above *London was heavily bombed during the Blitz. Over a million homes were damaged or destroyed, and almost 21,000 people killed. However, without the success of Operation Double Cross, the damage would have been much worse.*

TIMELINE 1940-1941

OCTOBER 1940
The German Air Force fails to destroy the British Royal Air Force in the Battle of Britain.

DECEMBER 1940
US codebreakers, led by William Friedman, break Purple, Japan's diplomatic code.

MAY 1941
In Operation Primrose, British Royal Navy officers capture an Enigma machine and codebooks from a German U-Boat.

It also led them to believe that they were in control of a successful spy ring in Britain, and they dropped in more agents to join the ring – straight into the hands of Tate and MI5.

In 1944, Tate's fictional spy ring saved the lives of many Londoners. The German handlers asked their British agents for reports on the landing sites of their deadly V2 rockets, and Tate and his colleagues sent back reports that falsely indicated that the rockets weren't reaching their targets. Using the false information they had been given, the Germans adjusted the rockets' range and future V2s missed the densely populated centre of London. The Nazis were so convinced by Tate that they continued to be impressed with the intelligence their 'agents' were sending, even though it never actually gave them a military advantage. Towards the end of the war, the Nazi government actually awarded some Double Cross agents – including Schmidt – Germany's highest military honour, the Iron Cross!

THE ABWEHR IN AMERICA

If German espionage in Britain was a dismal failure, it was not much more successful in the United States. In the 1930s, the Abwehr had a US spy network of more than 30 agents, mostly German-born Americans, who passed the organisation information about technology and national defence. But in 1939, the Abwehr made a fatal mistake when they tried to blackmail loyal US citizen, William Sebold into becoming the ring's radio operator. He went straight to the FBI and became a double agent. For 16 months FBI agents watched and filmed each spy passing information to Sebold. The agents also provided false intelligence for Sebold to transmit. Then the FBI closed down the Abwehr operation and arrested every spy. It was a disaster for German Intelligence. They could no

Below *Admiral Wilhelm Canaris, the head of the Abwehr until 1944.*

Right *This German miniature camera allowed an agent to take photographs while pretending to check his watch. It used a circular, six-exposure film.*

Above *The battleship* West Virginia *burns after the Japanese attack on Pearl Harbor. More than 2,000 Americans died in the raid, making the US declaration of war against Japan inevitable.*

longer access information on US preparations for war, and the development of the technologies that would later defeat them.

SPYING FOR JAPAN

The 7 December 1941 attack on Pearl Harbor, Hawaii, by Japan, which pulled the United States into the war, took America completely by surprise. Japanese Intelligence had been preparing for it for a long time, however. As far back as 1935, Japan had recruited a German family to spy for them in Hawaii.

The Kühn family bought a house in Honolulu, filled with fine furniture and expensive artworks, a cottage overlooking the harbor, and a sailing boat. Large sums of money regularly appeared in their family bank account, although Dr Bernard Kühn had no job. Each one of the Kühns played a role in this family spy ring. Mother Friedel and daughter Ruth opened a beauty salon where most of their talkative customers were the wives of high-ranking naval officers. Attractive, outgoing Ruth dated American sailors, eventually becoming engaged to a young officer. Dr Kühn and Friedel took many walks in the mountains above Pearl Harbor, and they always had a pair of powerful binoculars with them. They sailed around the harbour in their boat, making notes of everything they saw. Dr Kühn regularly took his ten-year-old son, Eberhard for walks along the waterfront, and the officers of warships sometimes invited the boy onboard for a tour of the vessel. The naval officers thought that the boy was asking questions out of curiosity, but the reality was more sinister. Eberhard had been trained to ask significant

Remember Pearl Harbor on a beautiful morn,
Remember Pearl Harbor and what came with the dawn.
A foe lighted on us with bombs bursting in air,
But they couldn't beat us for our flag was still waving there.
Our Army and Navy just fought with all their might,
And our planes from the air shot the foe right out of sight.
Remember Pearl Harbor, remember-
And the boys who died for liberty.

♫   *'Remember Pearl Harbor' by Johnny Noble.*

Right *In WWII, an agent's radio was commonly concealed in a suitcase. Discovery by the enemy could mean death for the agent. This example is from the United States.*

JUNE 1941
Nazi Germany invades the Soviet Union, as predicted by Magic intelligence. The invasion breaks a secret non-aggression pact between the two countries.

AUGUST 1941
The assassination of a German naval cadet is the first violent act of resistance in France.

questions, and when the two got home from these tours, Friedel noted down the answers.

THE DIPLOMAT SPY

Japanese spy, Takeo Yoshikawa was sent to Hawaii to assist the family. Yoshikawa set to work gathering intelligence: he found out when battleships arrived and left the harbour, went swimming to assess the water's depth and to note underwater obstructions, took boat trips to see if there were protective nets in the water, and observed US patrol planes to learn their schedules. The tireless work carried out by the Kühns and Yoshikawa enabled the Japanese to make their attack on Pearl Harbor as destructive as possible. Soon after the attack, the Kühn family's role was discovered, and all but little Eberhard were imprisoned. Yoshikawa's role was not discovered immediately, and he was able to return to Japan where he continued to work in naval intelligence.

Left *German-born doctor, Bernard Kühn recruited his entire family into a spy ring that helped Japan prepare for its devastating attack on Pearl Harbor.*

JOINT RESOLUTION Declaring that a state of war exists between the Imperial Government of Japan and the Government and the people of the United States and making provisions to prosecute the same.

Whereas the Imperial Government of Japan has committed unprovoked acts of war against the Government and the people of the United States of America:

Therefore be it Resolved by the Senate and House of Representatives of the United States of America in Congress assembled,

That the state of war between the United States and the Imperial Government of Japan which has thus been thrust upon the United States is hereby formally declared;

and the President is hereby authorized and directed to employ the entire naval and military forces of the United States and the resources of the Government to carry on war against the Imperial Government of Japan;

and, to bring the conflict to a successful termination, all of the resources of the country are hereby pledged by the Congress of the United States.

Congressional Declaration of War on Japan 8 December 1941.

Above *Alan Turing, the mathematical genius who did the most to break the German code Enigma.*

During World War II most of the messages that passed between war officials were transmitted by radio. The messages were transmitted in code so that they appeared meaningless to eavesdroppers. That was nothing new – codes have been used for centuries to keep information private. But now complex machines were being used to create the codes, and these codes seemed unbreakable. The new science of cryptanalysis was born to break the new codes. At the same time, intelligence organisations were seeking ways of making their country's messages secure against the enemy's codebreakers.

BLETCHLEY PARK CODEBREAKERS

In 1939, a British codebreaking organisation, Government Communications Headquarters (GCHQ), was moved to a Victorian mansion called Bletchley Park outside London and given the mission to intercept and break the German codes. A huge team was needed for this task, and Britain's universities were searched for mathematics and language experts. A brilliant young mathematician, Alan Turing, was among them. When the recruiters had used up all the resources that they could find in Britain's universities, they turned to less conventional methods, such as recommendations from friends or colleagues. They noticed that the

"No mention whatsoever may be made either in conversation or correspondence regarding the nature of your work. It is expressly forbidden to bring cameras etc. within the precincts of Bletchley Park (Official Secrets Act).

DO NOT TALK AT MEALS. There are the waitresses and others who may not be in the know regarding your own particular work.

DO NOT TALK TRAVELLING. Indiscretions have been overheard on Bletchley platform. They do not grow less serious further off.

DO NOT TALK IN THE BILLET. Why expect your hosts who are not pledged to secrecy to be more discreet than you, who are?

Excerpt from the series of regulations for Bletchley Park employees.

Above *This Victorian mansion, called Bletchley Park, became the centre for British codebreaking during World War II. It is now a museum.*

📽 FILM EXCERPT 📄 DOCUMENT 🎤 INTERVIEW/BOOK EXTRACT 🎵 SONG/POEM

cryptanalysts were often excellent chess players and puzzle solvers, and they set up a competition in a daily newspaper in which fans of a famously difficult crossword were asked to finish the puzzle in 12 minutes. Those who managed it received a letter inviting them for interview. Eventually, the Bletchley Park team was assembled.

ENIGMA – THE PERFECT CIPHER MACHINE?

The Germans mostly used a cipher machine called Enigma to encrypt their messages. In the 1920s, the German military had modified Enigma several times, making it more and more complicated. By the outbreak of war, the Nazis were convinced that Enigma was completely secure, and with good reason. Enigma used three rotors (wheels) and a plugboard to encrypt messages. When a letter was typed on the Enigma keyboard, a rotor automatically substituted another letter for it. When that same letter was typed again, a different letter was substituted for it. After 26 letters had been typed, the first rotor returned to its starting place and the second rotor began to operate, one letter at a time. Each rotor was wired differently from the other, so that it produced different substitutions.

Left A scene from the 2001 film Enigma, which fictionalised the story of the breaking of the German code at Bletchley Park.

TIMELINE 1941-1942

OCTOBER 1941
Ultra intelligence enables Allied air forces to sink five supply ships headed to assist Rommel's African campaign.

DECEMBER 1941
Camp X opens in Ontario, Canada for paramilitary training of secret agents. Japanese attack on Pearl Harbor brings the United States into WWII.

MAY 1942
The first Navajo recruits develop a code based on their language.

Above *The Nazi invasion of Poland in 1939 catapulted Europe into war and created a new urgency for the codebreaking efforts of the Allies and their friends.*

Right *This statue was erected in Bydgoszcz, Poland, to commemorate the brilliant mathematician and codebreaker Marian Rejewski.*

The plugboard, which contained wiring and jacks, or plugs, provided yet another level of encryption, by swapping letters again. Furthermore, the plugboard and rotors could be set to different positions, changing the ciphers again. Operators re-set them, sometimes every day, to pre-arranged positions that were set out in codebooks issued to the military. To read an Enigma message, an operator needed an identical machine set to exactly the same positions. Enigma used more than a million different ciphers before it repeated one. This cipher machine was certainly impenetrable – or so it seemed. But the Germans' confidence about Enigma's security did not allow for two possibilities: theft and human error.

BREAKING ENIGMA

The most significant codebreaking theft was carried out before the war by a spy called Hans-Thilo Schmidt, an employee of Germany's Cipher Office. In the 1920s, the Polish government had begun an intelligence gathering operation to try to discover Nazi Germany's military aims. As part of this operation a team of young mathematicians, led by Marian Rejewski, was recruited in 1932 to break the Enigma code. The team had an Enigma machine but did not know how it had been modified. In a stroke of luck, Rejewski was passed stolen secret documents – operating instructions and lists of Enigma settings – by Schmidt. These enabled Rejewski to build a replica Enigma called Bomba, which could decode messages. By 1938 Polish Intelligence was reading around 75 per cent of Germany's Enigma messages.

In 1939, with the Nazis poised to invade Poland, Polish Intelligence revealed everything they knew about Enigma to their British counterparts. With this help from the Polish team, and his own mathematical genius and knowledge of mechanical engineering, Alan Turing was able to produce an improved version of Rejewski's Bomba, called the Bombe. The Bombe could read Enigma settings up to a point, but a little human codebreaking was needed to narrow down the settings available to them. Codebreakers had to find a 'crib' – a bit of encrypted text that they could translate – to help the Bombe. A crib could be made from repeated words or phrases. The trick was finding chunks of phrasing that were repeated from message to message and that codebreakers could compare between messages. Luckily for the codebreakers, the Nazi operators often ended their messages patriotically with 'Heil Hitler'. 'Nothing to report' was also a common message. When codebreakers recognised these repeats, they had the clues they needed to break larger chunks of information. These repeats were the human error that helped break Enigma.

"In Hut 4, we worked with brilliant linguists from Oxford and Cambridge. When we received the German messages which had been decoded, they translated them from German into English, and then sent these to typists to be typed up. Then they were brought back, and we had to check them very carefully, with the handwritten translations, so that there were no typing errors. These decoded messages gave the positions of the U-boats out in the Atlantic, and so you can imagine that a number 3 altered to a number 5, and a number 6 altered to a number 8 could have fatal consequences; it could prove fatal to our shipping."

Diane Neal, a Bletchley Park employee.

ULTRA INTELLIGENCE

During the war, the Enigma codebreaking effort was assisted by further thefts of information. The codebooks, which typically showed one month's plugboard and rotor settings, were so valuable that secret operations were carried out just to steal them. The most successful was the top-secret Operation Primrose of 1941, in which a number of codebooks and an Enigma machine were recovered from a bombed U-boat. By 1945, there were more than 200 Bombes in operation. By the end of the war almost all the Enigma traffic transmitted by the German armed forces and by the intelligence organisation Abwehr was being read. The intelligence that came from the breaking of the Enigma codes was called Ultra. It was important in many campaigns of the war, particularly the Allied victory in the Battle of the Atlantic – the German attempt to sink Britain's supply ships. Ultra also helped British Intelligence find out if the misinformation it was transmitting through its double agents was being taken seriously by the enemy.

Right The Enigma cipher machine looked much like a typewriter with some extra features – a plugboard and rotors to encrypt messages.

PURPLE AND THE MAGICIANS

In 1939, Japanese Intelligence devised an even more fiendish cipher machine than Enigma, called Purple by the Americans. Although the United States had not yet joined the war, the US Army's Signal Intelligence Service (SIS) was given the task of breaking Purple. The SIS's head was a brilliant,

TIMELINE
1942-1945

27 MAY 1942
Reinhard Heydrich, chief of the Reich Security Main Office for the Nazis is assassinated by SOE agents in Prague, dying just over a week later.

Above *Reinhard Heydrich was assasinated by SOE agents.*

JULY 1942
President Roosevelt establishes the Office of Strategic Services (OSS) in the United States.

SEPTEMBER 1944
V2 rockets hit London but Operation Double Cross helps minimise damage to the capital.

Four female SOE agents, captured in France, are executed at Dachau Concentration Camp.

MARCH 1945
The United States captures the Japanese island of Iwo Jima, with help from the Navajo code talkers.

Above *Cryptanalyst Elizebeth Friedman, who introduced her husband William to cryptology.*

"A cipher is different from a code . . . The difference is a simple one, and can be put quite briefly. In code systems, the units or symbols to be translated can be of different lengths: a letter, a syllable, a word, a sentence, or just a string of letters or numbers is agreed to stand for a particular word or a whole phrase in the message (for example, 'A cat may look at a King' might be agreed to mean 'Oil shares steady'. . .). In contrast, the units in cipher systems are of uniform length and bear a uniform relationship to the units of the plain text. Usually one letter in the cipher corresponds to one letter in the message, though in some systems groups of two or even three letters are used in a cipher to stand for one letter in the message."

William and Elizebeth Friedman explain codes and ciphers in their book *The Shakespearian Ciphers Examined.*

Below *Operatives working on one of the Colossus machines at Bletchley Park, which were designed to decode German messages from Lorenz machines.*

pioneering codebreaker, William Friedman. He knew that only advanced mathematics had a chance of solving Purple, and all of his handpicked 12-person team were mathematical wizards – or magicians, as they became known. Under Friedman's leadership, the magicians became compulsive workers, even solving ciphers in their spare time. Friedman and his wife, who was also a devoted and accomplished codebreaker, held dinner parties for the magicians, and to attend they had to solve a cipher informing them of the

name of the restaurant and its address They sent each other Christmas and birthday cards in cipher, competing with one another to devise the most difficult puzzle.

Friedman and his magicians began studying intercepted Purple messages. They hoped that a mathematical analysis would give them clues about the type of cipher machine that had created the messages. It was a harder task than the Enigma team's. Not only did they have to work with the complex Japanese language, they also had no idea what type of cipher machine they were looking for. The magicians looked for cribs, and soon discovered that the Japanese operators numbered their messages and spelled out the encrypted number at the beginning of each message. This discovery enabled them to make progress in one area, but they were soon stumped again. A year of intense but monotonous work followed before the breakthrough they had all been waiting for finally came. In August 1940, magician Genevieve Grotjan found a pattern of relationships between ciphertext and plaintext. The team was overjoyed.

This discovery enabled more relationships to be plotted. From these, the magicians could work out how Purple operated. Leo Rosen, a former MIT electronics student, was able to build a replica Purple from the team's calculations. Rosen and a colleague finished wiring up the machine late one evening, and immediately fed it with a Purple ciphertext message. The plaintext was revealed. Purple was broken.

MAGIC INTELLIGENCE

By autumn 1940, Purple messages were being decrypted. The intelligence gained from Purple was called Magic, in honour of the magicians. Only Japan's diplomats used Purple machines – the Japanese armed forces used different cipher machines – so military messages could not be read. But Magic still proved a rich source of information. The pro-Nazi Japanese ambassador to Germany frequently had revealing conversations with Hitler himself. Through reports of these conversations transmitted by Purple, US Intelligence learned that the Nazis planned to invade the Soviet Union. This information was passed to Soviet leader Joseph Stalin but, ironically, he refused to believe it. At the end of the war, Magic revealed that Japan would not surrender even if threatened by invasion. It was this information that led to the dropping of atomic bombs on the Japanese cities of Hiroshima and Nagasaki.

Above This 'Purple' cipher machine was used by Japanese diplomats. Two similar Japanese machines were known by the colour codenames Coral and Jade.

Left Originally a Russian Jewish immigrant, William Friedman headed the team that broke Purple and became the United States' most famous codebreaker.

TIMELINE 1945-1948

MAY 1945
Germany formally surrenders, bringing an end to World War II and to fighting in Europe.

AUGUST 1945
Nuclear bombs are dropped on Hiroshima and Nagasaki, Japan, after Magic intelligence – and other sources – reveals that surrender is unlikely.

SEPTEMBER 1947
Central Intelligence Agency (CIA) established in the United States.

FEBRUARY 1948
The Soviet Union initiates a communist takeover of former Czechoslovakia.

JUNE 1948
The Blockade of Berlin begins with the Soviets blocking access to Western-occupied areas of the city.

ARTICLE 1. Japan recognizes and respects the leadership of Germany and Italy in the establishment of a new order in Europe.

ARTICLE 2. Germany and Italy recognise and respect the leadership of Japan in the establishment of a new order in Greater East Asia.

ARTICLE 3. Japan, Germany, and Italy agree to cooperate in their efforts on aforesaid lines. They further undertake to assist one another with all political, economic and military means if one of the Contracting Powers is attacked by a Power at present not involved in the European War or in the Japanese-Chinese conflict.

Excerpt from The Tripartite Pact made between Japan, Germany and Italy in 1940. An ally of the Axis powers, Japan was an intelligence target before it joined the war.

Above *The Sigaba cipher machine, created by the SIS, used many more rotors than Enigma, making it unbreakable.*

CODE TALKERS

Friedman's magicians were responsible for creating codes as well as breaking them. They devised a cipher machine called Sigaba that was used by the US Army and Navy throughout the war. Sigaba was never broken by the enemy, but Sigaba machines were too big and heavy to be used in the battlefield. Other systems were used for tactical communications, and the most successful of these was the Navajo code talkers. The code talkers did not need complicated cipher machines. They were able to communicate directly with one another in a verbal code on two-way radios and telephones.

In 1942, Area Signal Officer Lieutenant Colonel Jones, stationed in San Diego, California, received an intriguing proposal from an engineer, Philip Johnston. Johnston suggested that he could create a completely secure code for sending and receiving messages on the battlefield. The son of a missionary, Johnston had grown up on a Navajo reservation in Arizona in the early 1900s. He was one of just 30 non-Navajos to be able to speak the language. His idea for an unbreakable code was based on the use of this obscure and impenetrable tongue. There was one hitch – there were no Navajo words for many of the military terms that would be used in battlefield messages. But Johnston had a solution – Navajo recruits could create them. Jones was impressed and the scheme began. Recruiters visited the Navajo reservations in search of suitable candidates. Thirty were chosen, and these were

Right *Former Navajo code talker and US marine Dan Akee shows the Congressional Medal of Honor awarded to him for bravery during World War II.*

MILITARY TERM	NAVAJO WORD	NAVAJO MEANING
Battleship	Lo-tso	Whale
Aircraft Carrier	Tsidi-ney-ye-hi	Bird carrier
Submarine	Besh-lo	Iron fish
Mine Sweeper	Cha	Beaver
Destroyer	Ca-lo	Shark
Troop Transport	Dinch-nev-ye-hi	Man carrier
Cruiser	Lo-tso-yazzie	Small whale

Navajo code talkers' terms for ships.

enlisted into the US Marines. They underwent military and radio operating training before they began work on developing the code and creating the new terms. After a great deal of hard work the team announced their results. They created a list of more than 200 military terms. The name for Britain was 'bounded by water', and for Germany 'iron hat'. For the code, a Navajo noun, usually a plant or animal, stood for each letter of the alphabet. These first codemaker recruits were posted to Guadalcanal in the Solomon Islands. They were successful straight away, and a training programme was established for further recruits, with Johnston as course instructor.

Above *In the Pacific, a two-man team of Navajo code talkers relay orders over the field radio using their native language as the basis for their coded commands.*

The Navajo marines were regular troops as well as communications experts and runners (delivering messages by hand, often while dodging a hail of bullets). They were never used in Europe, but they took part in every battle in the Pacific against Japan and its allies. Fighting the Japanese caused them some trouble with their own side, however. Some of the Navajos appeared Asian to other US troops, leading to their being harassed or even arrested under suspicion of being Japanese spies. One Navajo soldier was assigned a bodyguard after almost being shot as a spy. The Navajos were effective in all the Pacific battles, but it was at Iwo Jima that they were most successful. Throughout the 35-day clash between US and Japanese forces, six code talkers worked around the clock. They sent and received more than 800 vital messages in the first two days of the battle alone. After the war, the code talkers' contribution was recognised as a vital factor in the US victory at Iwo Jima. In all, 420 Navajo code talkers served in the Marine Corps, of which 13 were killed. The Japanese never broke their code.

TIMELINE 1949-1953

APRIL 1949
NATO – a military alliance of 12 nations including the United States and Britain – is established.

OCTOBER 1949
The People's Republic of China is founded by Mao Zedong.

JUNE 1950
The Korean War begins when the Communist North, supported by the Soviet Union, invades the South.

APRIL 1953
Casino Royale, the first of 12 novels featuring fictional spy James Bond, is published.

19 JUNE 1953
Julius and Ethel Rosenberg executed for treason.

"The conventional code uses scrambled numbers and letters and it is scrambled—an ordinary message is written on a pad or a paper and given to an expert to scramble, to code. So when he's done he gives it to the radio operator and the radio operator sends it, and it's written down at the other end the way it is sent. And from there it goes to another expert and he unscrambles it. So there's time lost. If a Navajo code-talker is really fluent with his code system he is given a message, it's sent, he looks at it, calls the receiver on the other side: "Here's the message", and the receiver will say, "Go ahead and send it", or something like that, and he encodes them as he is talking and the guy over there is decoding it as he's saying it. Maybe it comes through a minute or two minutes. Ordinary messages are never more than three minutes, and when you're doing that you're saving lives."

President of the Navajo Code Talkers Association, Keith Little, remembers his time as a recruit.

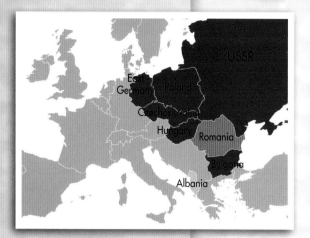

From the ashes of World War II, the United States and the Soviet Union – allies in the fight against the Axis – now squared off against one another on the world stage. As the world's two superpowers, they established alliances, or friendships, with other nations and prepared for battle.

Above This map shows the countries in the Soviet bloc – countries that were controlled by the USSR. Albania split with the USSR in the early 1960s but remained Communist. Although Romania did not split with the USSR, it maintained a much more independent stance than other countries within the Soviet bloc.

The North Atlantic Treaty Organization (NATO), was formed as a military alliance between the United States and the Western European democracies, which now would include the newly formed West Germany. The Soviet Union responded with the Warsaw Pact – an alliance that included the countries of Eastern Europe that had become communist 'satellites' of the Soviet Union following the war. One of these nations would be East Germany, also newly formed, but under the mantle of Soviet-style communism. But there was no military conflict. Instead a 'Cold War' endured between the two superpowers. In this Cold War, espionage played a vital role as each side jockeyed for political, economic, and military power – and prepared for battle in case the Cold War should ever become hot.

COMMUNIST PROMISE
Before World War II, when the Soviet Union was still a young nation, communism seemed to offer the possibility of a fairer society. In the 1930s, Britain and the United States alike had suffered under the period of economic crisis known as the Great Depression, which put many people out of work and into poverty. Communism held out hope for a classless society in which wealth would be shared equally between everyone. It was these hopes for a better, fairer society that led some people to

Below Donald Maclean, part of the infamous Cambridge Five spy ring.

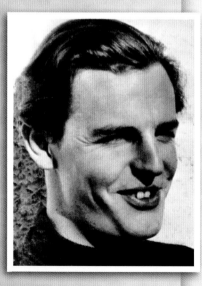

Above The USSR's top spy ring became known as the Cambridge Five because all were educated here, at Britain's prestigious Cambridge University.

MARCH 1954
The Soviet Union's security agency, the KGB, is established.

14 MAY 1955
The Warsaw Pact, a military alliance between communist states, is formed.

1961
Soviet double agent Kim Philby exposes British secret agent David Cornwell to the KGB. Cornwell turns to writing spy stories as John Le Carré.

AUGUST 1961
The Berlin Wall is built, preventing East Germans travelling to the West.

become spies for the Soviet Union. Among the most infamous of them were four friends – upper-class, wealthy Englishmen who became committed communists while attending Britain's highly regarded Cambridge University. They were Kim Philby (codename Stanley), Donald Maclean (codename Homer), Anthony Blunt (codename Johnson) and Guy Burgess (codename Hicks). After graduating from university, all four gained important posts in British Intelligence. Recruited during the 1930s, they began passing information to the Soviets during World War II and continued during the Cold War, becoming the most effective spy ring the Soviets ever had.

MACLEAN'S BRILLIANT CAREER

In 1944, Donald Maclean landed an important post at the British Embassy in Washington, and he soon became the Soviet Union's top spy. He attended top-secret meetings where note taking was forbidden, but he memorised the

Left Soviet Premier, Nikita Kruschev and US President Kennedy meet for crisis talks during the Cuban Missile Crisis of 1962. The crisis began after US spy planes took aerial photos of what looked like missile bases under construction in Cuba.

Below Guy Burgess, one of the Cambridge Five.

discussions and wrote them up later in the privacy of his home. These notes helped Soviet leader Stalin plan communist take-overs in Europe. In 1947, Maclean attended a conference about sharing wartime atomic secrets between some Western nations and was able to share many of them with the Soviet Union. Ironically, he became such a trusted diplomat that he was given a special pass to visit the Atomic Energy Commission alone, which even the director of the FBI was not allowed to do. With this pass Maclean was able to freely rifle through classified information about the development of the nuclear bomb. He had a near-photographic memory, and often memorised the contents of documents rather than use the miniature camera given to him to by his Soviet handler. Every week Maclean went to New York to make a 'dead drop' — leaving documents in a pre-arranged place to be picked up by his handler. He was able to make these trips without his bosses becoming suspicious because his American wife lived in New York.

> "While in government service he [Philby] carried out his duties ably and conscientiously, and I have no reason to conclude that Mr Philby has at any time betrayed the interests of his country, or to identify him with the so-called 'Third Man', if indeed there was one."
>
> *Statement from British foreign secretary Harold Macmillan in 1955, eight years before Philby was revealed as a spy and the 'third man' who tipped off Burgess and Maclean.*

PROJECT VENONA

But time would run out for Maclean. In 1946, a top-secret British-US codebreaking operation called Project Venona had been set up to decrypt messages sent by the Soviet Union's intelligence agencies. By 1950, the codenames of Soviet spies were becoming known, and one of them was Homer. It was found that Homer's messages were sent from New York. With this information, it was only a matter of time before Maclean was identified. But, luckily for the spy, the man assigned to discover Homer's identity was none other than his partner-in-crime Kim Philby. He of course warned Maclean, who immediately deserted Britain, defecting to Moscow and taking another member of the Cambridge spy ring, Guy Burgess, with him.

> ### 'Cambridge spies' surface in Moscow
> Two British diplomats who vanished in mysterious circumstances five years ago have reappeared in the Soviet Union. Guy Burgess and Donald Maclean handed a statement to four representatives from the press in a hotel room overlooking Moscow's Red Square. . . . [T]he former diplomats denied ever having been Soviet agents. They said they had come to the USSR to "work for the aim of better understanding between the Soviet Union and the West".
>
> In 1951 Guy Burgess and Donald Maclean were recalled to London from the British embassy in Washington after confidential documents went missing. . . . [A]fter their recall . . . both men disappeared before they could be questioned.
>
> At the time it was rumoured there was a "third man" who had tipped them off. Since then there has been continuing speculation about a spy ring composed of former Cambridge University students.
>
> *From the BBC Archives, 11 February 1956.*

THE ROSENBERGS UNCOVERED

Project Venona uncovered the codenames of an incredible 349 Soviet spies in the United States. Many of them would never be identified, but the codenames 'Liberal' and 'Antenna' led to an unassuming Jewish couple with two children, Julius and Ethel Rosenberg. Information from another source backed up Venona — Julius was running a spy ring for the Soviets and passing on classified information from his job in aeronautics. His wife typed up notes.

Above *Checkpoint Charlie was the most famous crossing point between East and West Berlin during the division of the Cold War. In 1989, after the fall of the Berlin Wall, the booth was taken to the Allied Museum in Berlin.*

TIMELINE 1962–1965

OCTOBER 1962
USSR builds missile bases in communist Cuba, only 144 km off Florida, causing the Cuban Missile Crisis. The US and USSR are closest to nuclear war than at any other time in the Cold War.

JANUARY 1963
Kim Philby defects to Moscow as he is about to be unmasked as a spy.

MARCH 1965
US involvement in the Vietnam War begins.

SEPTEMBER 1965
Get Smart, created by comedians Mel Brooks and Buck Henry, makes its first appearance on television.

DECEMBER 1965
The Spy Who Came in from the Cold, based on a novel by John Le Carré, appears in cinemas to critical acclaim.

Amid a storm of protest at the harshness of the sentence, the Rosenbergs became the only US citizens to be executed for espionage during the Cold War. Their two sons were adopted by a childless couple who were sympathetic to the communist cause. Today, most historians agree that the intelligence the Rosenbergs passed to the Soviets was of little value, but the same cannot be said for Maclean and his colleagues, none of whom were arrested. Philby provided information that led to the capture and deaths of dozens of British agents. But Maclean's spying was probably the most valuable for the Soviet Union. He helped Stalin build the Iron Curtain – the division of Europe into communist and democratic states – and advanced the Korean War.

SELLING AMERICA'S SECRETS

By the 1960s, the Soviet system had fallen out of favour with many in the United States who had once looked to Soviet communism as a just and fair way of distributing wealth. Spies who were willing to pass secrets to the Soviet intelligence and security agency known as the KGB because of their communist ideals were in short supply. But the days of the walk-in spy, who needed no encouragement, were not over. Prospective spies were still knocking on the KGB's door, but now they were in it for the money.

John Anthony Walker was a naval communications specialist, able to access secret messages between nuclear subs, orders to naval fleets and naval intelligence reports. His brother and son were also in the navy. Walker had no sympathy for communism but, when in 1967 a business venture failed, Walker became desperate for money. He walked into the Soviet Embassy in Washington, D.C., and offered

Right *Communist traitors Ethel and Julius Rosenberg are transported from court to prison after being found guilty of treason in 1951.*

Above *The espionage careers of John Walker and Aldrich Ames both began at the Soviet Embassy in Washington, D.C.*

classified information in exchange for several thousand dollars. Soon he was on the KGB payroll. Walker was given a miniature camera for photographing documents and instructions for a dead drop outside the city, so that he could leave documents and pick up cash without meeting an agent. By 1968 Walker was earning around $4,000 a month from his spying activities, but he realised he could be making even more money if he had his own spy ring. He set about recruiting a colleague, Jerry Whitworth, whom he knew was short of money. The pair passed top-secret information to the Soviets until the mid 1970s, when Whitworth backed out and Walker retired. Not wanting to kiss his fat KGB salary goodbye, Walker then recruited his own brother Arthur and son Michael. Walker continued making monthly dead drops on Arthur's and Michael's behalf until 1985, when his disgruntled ex-wife tipped off the FBI. Walker and the other members of the spy ring were soon arrested, and all but Michael received life sentences.

MILITARY AND HUMAN COST

In his 18 years of spying Walker helped the Soviets read more than 200,000 encrypted naval messages. As a result, the US military had to rebuild their entire communications network at a cost of around $1 billion. A year after Walker's arrest, CIA agent Aldrich Ames, his finances and personal life under enormous stress, walked into the Soviet Embassy in Washington and offered to sell secrets. The secrets he had to sell had less military value but a higher human cost than Walker's, for they were the identities of US agents in the Soviet Union. Soon after Ames became a Soviet spy, some of the CIA's Russian double agents were assassinated. Then, FBI agents began disappearing too and an investigation began. When Ames came under suspicion, he twice passed lie detector tests and convinced officers of his innocence. The investigation continued until around 1990, a KGB defector provided clues that again pointed to Ames who was immediately put under surveillance. When officers searched his house they found copies of reports he had written for the KGB, as well as documents showing payments made to him for the reports.

Left *John Anthony Walker (left) escorted by a law enforcement officer on his way to court to appear on espionage charges. He is currently serving a life sentence in prison.*

As a result of passing on the names, at least 10 US agents were assassinated, and around a hundred intelligence operations were unsuccessful. Ames received more than $4 million from the KGB, the most money a spy has ever made. He was finally arrested in 1994 and sentenced to life imprisonment.

AN IDEAL SPY

The traffic of classified information between the Soviet Union and the United States was by no means one-way. At the same time the United States was losing its secrets via spies such as Walker and Ames, it was also gaining Soviet secrets. The most important of them were coming from Dmitri Polyakov of the Soviet Military Intelligence organisation called the GRU. Polyakov was a Russian patriot and had no wish to defect to the United States, but he was disillusioned with the inequality and corruption in Soviet society, and wanted to give the United States an advantage in the Cold War. Around 1960, while working undercover as a diplomat in New York, Polyakov approached FBI officers who assigned him the codename 'Tophat'. For the next 25 years he worked as a US double agent while steadily rising up the ranks of Russian Intelligence, and gaining access to ever more valuable information. All that time, Polyakov did not accept a wage for his spying. His only payment was in the form of occasional gifts such as fishing gear and power tools. The first intelligence Polyakov gave the FBI was the names of four US soldiers and a British guided missile researcher who were selling military secrets to the Soviet Union. Later he became head of the GRU's China section and was able to obtain documents tracking the breakdown in the relationship between the Soviet Union and China. This understanding of the rivalry between the two communist powers helped persuade US president Richard M. Nixon that it would be in the United States's best interests to improve its relations with China in 1972.

Above *The logo of the GRU – the main intelligence agency of the Russian Federation.*

Left *Aldrich Ames stands in the dock where he was sentenced to life imprisonment for his espionage activities.*

JULY 1969
The United States wins the space race when Apollo 11 lands on the Moon.

FEBRUARY 1972
US president Richard M. Nixon meets communist chairman Mao Zedong in China, beginning an era of diplomatic relations between the Western superpower and the Soviet Union's communist rival.

JULY 1975
The Apollo-Soyuz Test Project sees Soviet cosmonauts and American astronauts in space together.

DECEMBER 1979
USSR invades Afghanistan to support its crumbling communist regime.

MARCH 1980
US boycotts the Moscow Summer Olympics to protest the invasion of Afghanistan.

JUNE 1987
Soviet premier Mikhail Gorbachev announces perestroika and glasnost – policies aimed at openness and reform.

Above *Crowds of Berliners gather at the Brandenburg Gate on 10 November 1989, after the fall of the Berlin Wall unified Berlin.*

Below *General Dmitri Polyakov supplied information to the United States for 25 years. He was betrayed by both Aldrich Ames and Robert Hanssen and executed by the Soviets in 1986.*

FROM HERO TO TRAITOR

Polyakov had several ways to make dead drops secure. When photographing documents, he sometimes used a type of film that could be developed only with special chemicals that only he and his handlers knew about. Polyakov put the film inside fake hollow stones, which he left at dead drop sites in rural areas for his handlers. In 1974 Polyakov became a General and was able to provide his US handlers with a list of all the US military technology that Soviet spies were trying to steal. He was now so important to US Intelligence that making even carefully disguised dead drops was too great a security risk. So the CIA designed an ingenious communications device for him. Polyakov typed into the handheld device, which automatically encrypted the text. Then he took an ordinary public bus. As the bus passed the US embassy, he pressed a button on the device that transmitted the information to a receiver inside the embassy. Polyakov continued spying without arousing a hint of suspicion. But a few years after his retirement in 1980, he simply disappeared. Around 1990, the CIA discovered that agent Aldrich Ames had sold Polyakov's identity to the KGB. It is likely that the General received the punishment reserved for Soviet traitors – a bullet in the back of the head and burial in an unmarked grave.

POSTHUMOUS AWARD

A member of the United States Air Force (USAF), Francis Gary Powers' exceptional abilities as a pilot soon saw him recruited by the CIA to fly covert operations over enemy territory. In 1956, he joined the CIA U-2 programme. The U-2 was a spy plane that could reach altitudes of 80,000 feet allowing it to take aerial photographs of Soviet targets. It wasn't until 1960 that the Soviets developed anti-aircraft guns capable of shooting down targets at that height.

Shot down over the central Russian city of Sverdlovsk (now called Ekaterinaburg), on 1 May 1960, Powers was unable to

Right *Gary Powers, one of the most famous figures in the Cold War was killed on 1 August 1977 when his helicopter crashed in California.*

Above *The headquarters of the KGB in Moscow. It also housed the notorious Lubyanka prison where many Soviet dissidents were tortured and executed. It is now used by the FSB – the Russian equivalent of the FBI.*

self-destruct the plane and it landed intact – giving the Soviets proof that the US had been spying on them. After being held for several months, Powers made a confession and was sentenced to 10 years in prison. However, after just 21 months of his sentence, Powers was swapped for Soviet spy Vilyam Fisher (aka Rudolf Abel) and returned to a hostile reaction in the United States from people who thought he had betrayed secrets of the U-2 programme.

Cleared by a Senate Committee of any wrongdoing, Powers continued working as a pilot, but in the private sector. He was killed in August 1977 when the traffic helicopter he was flying ran out of fuel and crashed in California. Powers was posthumously awarded the Prisoner of War Medal and National Defense Service Medal in 2000.

TIMELINE 1988-1989

FEBRUARY 1988
Israeli whistleblower Mordecai Vanunu sentenced to 18 years imprisonment for treason and espionage after revealing Israel's nuclear weapons programme to the British press.

9-10 NOVEMBER 1989
The Berlin Wall dividing East and West Berlin is opened, paving the way for German reunification.

25 DECEMBER 1991
USSR is formally dissolved and all of its republics become independent nations, bringing the Cold War to an end. The Russian Federation is the largest and inherits most of the wealth and military power of the former Soviet Union.

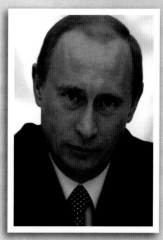

Above *Vladimir Putin, former President of the Russian Federation.*

POPULAR CULTURE SPY STORIES

QUIET!

LOOSE TALK
CAN COST LIVES

Above *One of many types of US World War II propaganda posters warning the public of the need for secrecy.*

During World War II, posters in city streets warned of enemy spies. With the war's end, the heroic exploits of the shadow army became known and were celebrated in the cinema. Cold War espionage literature introduced a new, morally divided spy and, in the 1960s, spy stories entered the world of comedy in a variety of guises. Today, serious and comic spies feature in a variety of popular culture forms. Not just films and books but also museums, board and digital games, and some children's toys are based on spy gadgets.

PROPAGANDA AND SPIES

World War II governments set up propaganda departments to warn people about the possibility of enemy spies in their midst. Well-known illustrators were commissioned to produce posters advising people that silence was the best policy. In Britain people were reminded that 'careless talk costs lives', and in the United States citizens were told to 'keep it under your Stetson' (a type of hat), and that 'loose lips sink ships'. In 1942, the message found its way into the cinema via Britain's Ealing Studios. In *The Next of Kin*, Nazi Intelligence uses spies to gather information from overheard conversations, and pieces the scraps together to uncover the

plans for an attack on German territory. So people were made aware of enemy spies, although they knew nothing of the real espionage operations carried out by their own governments.

WORLD WAR II STORIES

With the end of the war, the spies' stories could be told, and they were irresistible material for filmmakers. Many were so remarkable that they did not need any cinematic exaggerations,

Left *Scottish actor Sean Connery was the star of seven James Bond films between 1962 and 1983.*

"What the hell do you think spies are? Moral philosophers measuring everything they do against the word of God or Karl Marx? They're not! They're just a bunch . . . like me: little men, drunkards, . . . hen-pecked husbands, civil servants playing cowboys and Indians to brighten their rotten little lives. Do you think they sit like monks in a cell, balancing right against wrong?"

Excerpt from the script of the film of John Le Carré's The Spy Who Came in from the Cold.

Left *The 2001 film* Enigma *was based on a novel by Robert Harris which drew on the true story of the breaking of the Enigma code.*

> "It was part of his profession to kill people. He had never liked doing it and when he had to kill he did it as well as he knew how and forgot about it. As a secret agent who held the rare Double-O prefix — the licence to kill in the Secret Service — it was his duty to be as cool about death as a surgeon. If it happened, it happened. Regret was unprofessional — worse, it was a death-watch beetle in the soul."
>
> ***Excerpt from Chapter One of Bond novel* Goldfinger *by Ian Fleming.***

1998
Leo Marks, former head of Communications with the SOE, publishes his memoirs.

26 MARCH 2000
Ex-KGB officer Vladimir Putin becomes President of the Russian Federation.

SEPTEMBER 2000
Ex-MI5 officer and whistleblower David Shayler is charged with breaking Britain's Official Secrets Act after he reveals 'malpractice' at MI5 to the press.

SEPTEMBER 2001
The film *Enigma* tells a fictionalised story of the Bletchley Park codebreakers.

11 SEPTEMBER 2001
Attacks on the World Trade Center and the Pentagon highlighted a renewed need for international espionage.

and the films were made in a semi-documentary style. The war had barely ended when the story of FBI double agent William Sebold appeared as *The House on 92nd Street*. Real FBI agents played themselves, and FBI head J. Edgar Hoover appeared in the introduction. Similarly, in a film about a female spy, *Odette*, the head of the SOE, Maurice Buckmaster, appeared as himself. The World War II codebreakers would not get their fictional outing for a very long time. Incredibly, Bletchley Park employees were forbidden from talking about their wartime work until 1975. This was so that their efforts could be called upon again, if they were ever needed. Once this long period of silence had ended, their accounts, like those of their wartime comrades, the spies, appeared first as real-life accounts, then were fictionalised into popular stories.

COLD WAR SPIES IN FICTION

Espionage was the most important weapon of the long Cold War and, as real-life spies grew in numbers, spy stories multiplied too. In the novels of ex-spies Graham Greene and John Le Carré, spies became the subjects of serious literature. Their books explored the moral dilemmas that Cold War spies faced and asked whether it was

Left *A stamp featuring the covers of Ian Fleming's* From Russia with Love *novel which went on sale in 2008 to mark the 100th anniversary of the author's birth.*

I can tell you the license plate numbers of all six cars outside. I can tell you that our waitress is left-handed and the guy sitting up at the counter weighs two hundred fifteen pounds and knows how to handle himself.
I know the best place to look for a gun is the cab of the gray truck outside, and at this altitude, I can run flat out for a half mile before my hands start shaking. Now why would I know that? How can I know that and not know who I am?

Matt Damon's character Jason Bourne in the movie The Bourne Identity.

possible for a spy to be a good person. The world appeared more complex in the Cold War than it had during World War II, when the enemy – Nazi Germany, Japan, and their allies – was clearly wicked and the fight all too brutal. In the era of the Cold War, simple good versus evil stories seemed old-fashioned. But they lived on in the light-hearted James Bond action stories. In the 1950s and '60s, ex-Naval Intelligence Officer Ian Fleming wrote 12 novels and two books of short stories featuring British spy James Bond, whose Cold War enemies, many of them Soviet agents, were easily as wicked as the most evil enemies of all in World War II Europe – the Nazis. Although Bond is probably more handsome and cultured, and certainly luckier, than any real-life spy, many of the features of his world are true to life. Author Fleming used his own experiences as a spy to write the novels, and the types of gadgets Bond uses – as well as the chain of command in British Intelligence, Bond's relationship with the CIA and the use of codes for transmitting secret information – are all based on fact. The mixture of fantasy and fact was a winning combination, making Fleming a bestselling author and his creation James Bond the star of more than 20 films.

JOHN LE CARRÉ
TINKER TAILOR SOLDIER SPY
'A great thriller, the best le Carré has written'
Spectator

Above *John Le Carré's 1974 novel drew on the story of the Cambridge Five spy ring, with its main character closely based on Kim Philby.*

Right *A scene from the movie* Mission: Impossible *showing Tom Cruise using his skills to break into a high-security room within the CIA to steal a list detailing the identities of all their undercover agents.*

SPIES ON THE SILVER SCREEN

Today, espionage is more popular than ever before, especially among young people. It is starting to be represented in museums – the city of Washington, D.C., is home to an International Spy Museum. A huge range of mock spy gadgets, from invisible ink to wireless tracking systems, are available as children's toys. In the film *Spy Kids* the World War II organisation OSS (Office of Strategic Services) reappears but now it employs children too!

Uniting two of Hollywood's biggest stars – Brad Pitt and Angelina Jolie – *Mr and Mrs Smith* was a huge box-office hit around the world. The film centres on a married couple of spies who are both unaware of the other's secret life. Their undercover existence is so successful that they find each other dull, until they discover they are actually working for rival companies, and find themselves working against each other as they desperately try to survive.

Originally a hugely popular television series that aired between the 1960s and 1980s, *Mission: Impossible* made the successful move to the big screen in 1996 and has been followed by three sequels. Featuring a team of highly skilled secret agents, the Impossible Missions Force (IMF) use incredible high-tech gadgets and disguises to carry out their missions. They often used devices to disguise their voices and masks which were highly realistic- at the end of the missions, these masks were pulled off to reveal a member of the IMF team.

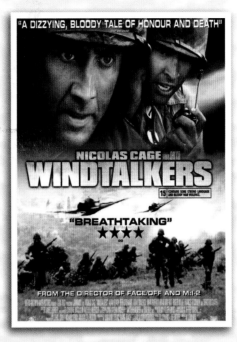

"A DIZZYING, BLOODY TALE OF HONOUR AND DEATH"

NICOLAS CAGE
WINDTALKERS

15

"BREATHTAKING"
★★★★

FROM THE DIRECTOR OF FACE/OFF AND M:I-2

Above *The film* Windtalkers *used non-Navajo stars to tell the story of the Navajo code talkers.*

Windtalkers is an action film about the Navajo code talkers used by the US Army against the Japanese in the Pacific. Directed by John Woo, who also directed the box-office hit *Mission: Impossible II*, the film is set around the battle for Saipan. It drew heavy criticism for focusing on the characters of the US soldiers assigned to protect them, rather than on the code talkers themselves. Originally planned for release in late 2001, the terrorist attacks of September 11 pushed back the release date by almost a year.

Could You Be a Spy?

Operation Spy at the International Spy Museum. It's a live-action spy adventure. You don't read about spies. You ARE the spy. You have one hour to locate a missing nuclear trigger before it ends up in the wrong hands. This is not an exhibit, it's as close to the real thing as you can get. Move quickly and think fast. Conduct surveillance. Polygraph a suspect agent. Steal secrets. Just don't screw up. Ready?

Advertisement for an experience, Operation Spy, at the International Spy Museum in Washington, United States.

CHAPTER 5

LATEST DEVELOPMENTS ESPIONAGE NOW

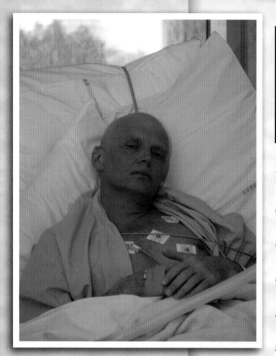

Above *Former KGB agent Alexander Litvinenko was forced to live in secret in London as a political refugee, and feared for his life. In November 2006, he fell ill. It is now believed that he was poisoned by a cup of tea contaminated with polonium-210, a radioactive substance. Litvinenko claimed that former KGB agents, directed by the Russian government, were responsible. He died on 23 November 2006. Extradition requests from Britain for the chief suspect, Andrei Lugovoi, have been refused by Russia.*

Below *Robert Hanssen is arrested shortly after making his final dead drop.*

In 1991, the Soviet Union was dissolved, bringing the Cold War to a dramatic finish. A nation of 16 republics collected into a single communist nation known officially as the Union of Soviet Socialist Republics (USSR) was now a group of independent nations. Most of them aspired to be democratic. The largest of these former republics – and the most important in the Soviet Union in terms of language, culture, and centre of government – was Russia. Despite the new, democratically elected government in Russia, however, the United States and the new Russian Federation continued to spy on one another as much as before.

Meanwhile, the world of espionage has been undergoing significant changes. A new sort of spy called a whistleblower has come on the scene. Economic spies are helping their countries compete with other nations for wealth. The computer revolution has made spying a whole lot easier, and given it frightening new possibilities.

OLD HOSTILITIES CONTINUE

The man appointed to run Russia's post–Cold War spy programme, Sergei Tretyakov, was himself working for the FBI. In 2000, he defected to the US and resettled with his family in a secret location under a new name. In 2001, a senior FBI agent, Robert Hanssen, was discovered to have been spying first for the KGB, then its successor the SVR, for most of his career. The end of communism appears to have made little difference to the level of espionage between the two nations, or to the motives of the spies, which usually involve some dissatisfaction with their own government and the lure of money.

WHISTLEBLOWER OR SPY?

A whistleblower is someone who reveals a secret to the press because he or she believes it should be out in the open. Political whistleblowers are usually treated as spies by the country whose secrets they have exposed. One of the most important whistleblowers was an Israeli, Mordechai Vanunu. In the 1980s, Israel publicly denied it was building nuclear weapons but, as engineer at the country's Nuclear Research Centre, Vanunu knew otherwise. He believed it was in the best interests of peace in the Middle East for the world to know that the Israeli government had a nuclear weapons programme. Before he left his government job in 1985, Vanunu took around 60 photographs, which clearly showed nuclear bomb-making materials at the research centre. In London, Vanunu gave a detailed interview, and passed the photographs, to Britain's leading newspaper, *The Sunday Times.*

The newspaper's editor insisted on verifying Vanunu's story with nuclear experts, and there was a delay of a few weeks before publication. Hanging around in London, Vanunu fell for a pretty American tourist, Cindy, whom he met by chance. When she invited him to her sister's empty apartment in Rome he didn't look back. But no sooner had he arrived than he was knocked unconscious, drugged, and smuggled onto a cargo ship

Left *Mordecai Vanunu spent 18 years in prison in Israel for revealing secrets of its nuclear capability to a newspaper in 1986.*

Hidden beneath the Negev desert, the factory has been producing atomic warheads for the last 20 years. Now it has almost certainly begun manufacturing thermo-nuclear weapons, with yields big enough to destroy entire cities.

Information about Israel's capacity to manufacture the bomb come from the testimony of Mordechai Vanunu, a 31-year-old Israeli who worked as a nuclear technician for nearly 10 years in Machon 2 – a top secret, underground bunker built to provide the vital components necessary for weapons production at Dimona, the Israeli nuclear research establishment.

Vanunu's testimony and pictures, ...show that Israel has developed the sophisticated and highly classified techniques needed to build up a formidable nuclear arsenal.

Excerpt from The Sunday Times, 5 October 1986 which revealed Mordecai Vanunu's top-secret revelations.

TIMELINE 2008

MAY 28, 2008
Sebastian Faulks' James Bond novel *Devil May Care* is published. This is the same date as the centenary of Ian Fleming's birth.

2008
Documents relating to persons involved with the OSS are released. Among those revealed to have been agents for OSS are celebrity chef Julia Child, actor Sterling Hayden, and the son of author Ernest Hemingway.

Below *The Negev Nuclear Research Centre in the desert south of Dimona, Israel. Vanunu worked here as a technician between 1976 and 1985.*

> "But the thing that most annoyed me was that I had positive intentions for what I did but the state turned me into a monster. I could not bear the thought that their reason for doing these things was simple revenge. I wanted to save the population of Israel from the disaster of a nuclear war and they turned me into a traitor and a spy. There was no proportion between my act and my punishment."

Mordecai Vanunu, speaking to the press from prison in 1998, after serving the longest known term of solitary confinement – 11 years.

Above *China has been accused of using economic espionage to accelerate its growing economy and modernise its cities, such as Shanghai.*

Right *At the height of the Cold War in 1968, a supersonic passenger jet took to the skies of the Soviet Union shortly before the maiden flight of Concorde. The Tu-144, which was quickly nicknamed 'Concordski' in the West, bore a remarkable resemblance to its Anglo-French supersonic rival, the Concorde. According to papers smuggled out of Russia by dissident KGB officer Vasili Mitrokin, specifications on new aircraft such as Concorde were stolen by a spy codenamed 'Ace'. The Tu-144's commercial future ended after one of the planes crashed at the Paris Air Show in 1973, killing 13 people.*

bound for Israel. Cindy was no American tourist. She was an agent of the Israeli Secret Service, Mossad. Somehow, Mossad had found out about Vanunu's conversations with journalists. Mossad did not want to damage Israel's relationship with Britain by arresting him there, so it hired 'Cindy' to lure him to Italy. Back in Israel, Vanunu was sentenced to 18 years imprisonment for espionage and treason. After serving his full sentence – an incredible eleven and a half years of it in solitary confinement – he was released in 2004, but forbidden to speak to the press.

ECONOMIC ESPIONAGE

Today, spies are more likely to be stealing economic secrets than political ones. Economic espionage has become a way of boosting the growth of a country's economy, and many of these new economic spies are working for foreign governments. It is easier to steal secrets today than it has ever been. Now, almost all information is stored digitally (electronically and in computers). This means that the days of stuffing documents into briefcases, or carefully photographing pages of text, are mostly over. Usually, the economic spy works for the targeted company and has access to important information in its internal computer network. He or she can copy vast amounts of information in seconds, from one computer's hard drive to another. Passing information is much faster and safer than it used to be too. In the past, the most dangerous part of a spying operation was making the dead drop. Several Cold

Above *Vanunu reveals his abduction by Mossad to journalists, using an ingenious method – it's written on his hand – as he is transported to prison.*

War spies were caught passing information to their handlers. Now spies – like the rest of us – use the Internet to send messages and information around the world in seconds. Unlike us, they may disguise the data with encryption techniques, and mask the identity of the recipient or sender.

CYBER ESPIONAGE

Spies may still have to work in an organisation to gain access to that information, but today it is possible to steal information from far away. Much of it is freely available on the Internet. This type of non-secret information is called open source intelligence. When the information sought is secret, computer hackers can use new codebreaking techniques to break into the computer systems of private companies and government organisations. In just one example, in 2008, investigators discovered that information was being moved from computers in the German government onto computers in China. In the future, sabotaging computer networks could be a greater threat than stealing information from them. Hacker terrorists could bring an entire city to a standstill by wrecking the computer networks that control important services, like electricity. The September 11 attacks have given the world's spies and codebreakers a new and urgent target. If spies can infiltrate terrorist groups such as al-Qaeda they may be able to prevent future attacks. The codemakers, or computer programmers, can help stop them too, by making computer networks secure against hackers.

"You can discuss the time and route of your trip to China with Mr. Mak in person. ... You may use 'travelling to Hong Kong' or 'visiting relatives in China' as reasons for travelling abroad. ... Normally, if you have any information, you can also pass it on to me through Mr. Mak. This channel is much safer than the others."

From a 2 May, 1987, letter by a handler to one of his spies, making arrangements for passing economic secrets to China.

The [British] Government has openly accused China of carrying out state-sponsored espionage against vital parts of Britain's economy, including the computer systems of big banks and financial services firms.

In an unprecedented alert, the Director-General of MI5 sent a confidential letter to 300 chief executives and security chiefs at banks, accountants and legal firms this week warning them that they were under attack from "Chinese state organisations". It is believed to be the first time that the Government has directly accused China of involvement in web-based espionage.

The Times, 1 December 2007.

ALAN TURING (1912-1954)

During World War II Alan Turing led a team at Bletchley Park, England, in deciphering messages encrypted by the German cipher machine Enigma. With the help of codebreaking work already carried out in Poland, Turing built a deciphering machine, the Bombe, for reading Enigma-coded messages. After the war he worked on the development of artificial intelligence and the first computers. In 1952 Turing was arrested for homosexuality, then illegal in Britain, and committed suicide two years later.

VIRGINIA HALL (1906-1982)

A native of Baltimore, Virginia Hall moved to Europe to study languages as a teenager. She became a hugely successful wartime spy and, after the war, a CIA analyst. Hall was posted to German-occupied France twice, first for Britain and then the United States. She established resistance networks and helped train resistance fighters in sabotage techniques, while also transmitting valuable intelligence on German army activities. After the war, Hall was honoured in both Britain and the United States.

WILLIAM FRIEDMAN (1891-1969)

Friedman was born to a Russian Jewish family that came to the United States in 1893. During World War I he became a codebreaker for the government, a role he stayed in until he retired in 1956. In the 1930s, Friedman and mathematician Frank Rowlett designed an unbreakable cipher machine called SIGABA, which the US military used in World War II. In 1939, given the task of breaking a new Japanese cipher called Purple, Friedman's team built a replica of Purple that enabled the US to read Japanese diplomatic messages.

ADMIRAL CANARIS (1887-1945)

Canaris was head of the German Intelligence organisation, the Abwehr, from 1935-1944. At first he supported Hitler but, after witnessing Nazi atrocities, he began to secretly work against his paymasters. He advised Spain's fascist leader, General Francisco Franco, not to allow Nazi troops into his country, tried to stop the Nazi invasion of Czechoslovakia, and attempted to negotiate peace with the Allies. Canaris personally saved hundreds of Jews from the concentration camps by pretending they were Abwehr agents. After a plot to assassinate Hitler failed, Canaris's double life was discovered. He was hanged at a concentration camp just two weeks before it was liberated by the Allies.

IAN FLEMING (1908-1964)

Ian Fleming was raised as a typical member of the English upper class. During World War II, he was recruited to Naval Intelligence, under the codename 17F. He became head of a successful intelligence-gathering outfit called 30 Assault Unit. Its members, trained in lock-picking, safe-cracking, and unarmed combat, went into enemy territory to steal items such as codebooks and radio and radar equipment. After the war Fleming used his experiences in Intelligence to create a fictional spy, James Bond. His 12 novels were turned into hugely popular films, making James Bond and his codename – 007 – instantly recognised all over globe.

PEARL CORNIOLEY (1914-2008)

Pearl Cornioley joined the British Special Operations Executive (SOE) in 1943 and, after seven weeks training in combat and sabotage, was dropped by parachute into occupied France. She worked as a courier for a resistance network until its leader was captured. She then became leader of another network and took charge of 1,500 resistance fighters. Under her leadership, they carried out many acts of sabotage against Nazi Germany, such as blowing up railway lines, to prevent troops from reaching the battlefields. Cornioley was so successful that Germany offered one million francs for her capture, but she survived the war and married a resistance fighter.

ALLEN DULLES (1893-1969)

Dulles is best known for being director of the CIA from 1953-1961, but in his early life he ran a successful spy ring against the Nazis. Dulles entered the diplomatic service aged 23 and worked in Austria, Switzerland, and Germany, partly as an intelligence gatherer. In 1942 he became chief of the Berne station of the Office of Strategic Services – in charge of recruiting spies in Switzerland and gathering intelligence from them. His network of spies included Abwehr double agents, and from them he was able to report on the activities of the German resistance. His most valuable recruit was diplomat Fritz Kolbe, who supplied thousands of secret Nazi documents.

KIM PHILBY (1912-1988)

A high-ranking British Intelligence officer, Philby was actually a Soviet double agent. He was a member of a spy ring sometimes called the Cambridge Five – because the five became communists while students of Cambridge University – with Guy Burgess, Donald Maclean, Anthony Blunt, and John Cairncross. Philby expressed pro-Nazi views to make him seem an unlikely communist and, in 1944, he became head of counterespionage against the Soviets, a perfect position for protecting himself and his fellow double agents. However, Philby began to attract suspicion and in 1963 he defected from Britain to the Soviet Union. In 1968 he published his autobiography, *My Silent War*. Philby was responsible for the deaths of hundreds of British agents.

ANTHONY BLUNT (1907-1983)

Blunt was the most senior member of the Cambridge Five, and helped to recruit Anthony Burgess and Donald Maclean. During World War II he worked for MI5, and was able to pass on Ultra intelligence from intercepted Enigma messages to the Soviet Union. After the war he started a career as an art historian, becoming so successful that he was appointed Surveyor of the Queen's Pictures – in charge of the royal family's art collection. He even received a knighthood, making him Sir Anthony Blunt. In 1963 MI5 discovered his espionage, but it was kept secret until 1979. After that, Blunt was stripped of his knighthood but he was never brought to trial for his spying.

ELIZABETH BENTLEY (1908-1963)

Born in Connecticut, Elizabeth Bentley studied in Florence, Italy, where she became interested in fascism. She soon changed allegiances and in 1935 she joined the Communist Party of the United States of America (CPUSA). In New York City, she became a courier for a Soviet agent, Jacob Golos, taking documents and messages from his network of American spies. When he suddenly died, she took over the network. But in 1945, as she was about to be unmasked, Bentley approached the FBI and offered to become an informer. She gave the FBI the names of more than 100 Soviet spies, among them Julius Rosenberg.

OLEG PENKOVSKY (1919-1963)

A Colonel in the Soviet military intelligence organisation the GRU, Penkovsky was also a double agent known to his handlers by the codename Agent Hero. In 1961 Penkovsky began passing important MI6 and CIA documents about Soviet weapons development. His Moscow contact was a female British spy, Janet Chisholm – the mother of three young children. Penkovsky would meet Chisholm in a local Moscow park and pass her documents and photographs, which she would hide in her baby's pram. In October 1962 the KGB learned about Penkovsky's spying from one of its double agents. He was immediately arrested and was executed some months later.

JUAN PUJOL (1912-1988)

World War II Spanish double agent, Juan Pujol is one of the few people to have received military decorations from both Britain and Germany. Around 1940, Pujol became a German spy by pretending to be living in Britain (he was actually in Portugal), and in control of a network of agents. Once he was trusted by Abwehr, he offered his services to British Intelligence. Soon he really was in Britain and operating as a double agent (codename Garbo). He passed misinformation to the Nazis for the rest of the war, and was instrumental in the plot to convince the Germans that the Normandy landings would take place elsewhere. After the war he moved to Venezuela.

GLOSSARY

Abwehr The German intelligence organisation which existed from 1922-1944.

Agent Another word for spy. May also be called secret agent, or intelligence officer.

Allied Powers Those nations allied against the Axis, primarily Britain, the Soviet Union and the United States.

Axis Powers Germany, Italy, Japan and other countries opposed to the Allied Powers.

Cipher Different to a code, a cipher uses letters as symbols that stand for other letters to create apparently meaningless patterns of letters. The message is known only by those who understand what the words or symbols mean.

Cipher machine Electromechanical device for creating millions of different ciphers.

Ciphertext Text that has been encrypted with a cipher machine, so that it appears meaningless.

Classified Information that has been officially designated as confidential or secret.

Code The substitution of certain words or numbers for different ones which disguise the true contents of that message.

Codename The name by which a spy is known to his or her handler and intelligence agency. If a spy works with more than one agency, they will have a number of different codenames.

Code talker Someone who can speak in code. In World War II, Navajo marines acted as code talkers so that the Japanese would not be able to decipher the messages.

Communism An economic and political system in which wealth is owned collectively by the people through the state.

Counterespionage Activity that aims to prevent or work against enemy espionage.

Counterintelligence Activity to prevent enemy intelligence agencies from gathering information.

Covert Hidden or secret. Spies may be said to operate covertly when they are under cover.

Cryptanalysis The science of decrypting text, also called codebreaking.

Dead drop A prearranged place to exchange secret information and payment for the information.

Decrypt to convert encrypted text to plaintext.

Defect To desert one country for another. During the Cold War a number of Soviets defected to Western countries, and communist sympathisers defected to the USSR.

Democracy A nation that operates under the idea that the people hold the power to rule their own country, either directly or through their elected representatives.

Diplomat Someone appointed to represent his or her government abroad. Spies often operate under cover as diplomats.

Diplomatic relations Negotiation between the diplomats of different countries. To open diplomatic relations with a country is to make a friendly gesture.

Double agent A spy who is secretly working for the government they are spying on. Some double agents start off by working for their government's enemy, while others are persuaded or decide to, change their allegiance.

Encode To convert a plaintext message into a coded one.

Encrypt To convert plaintext to a code or cipher.

Enigma The name given to a German cipher machine used throughout World War II.

Espionage The use of spies to obtain secret information.

Guerrilla Warfare The name given to sabotage, raids, and other acts of combat carried out by a small group against a formal army.

Hacker Someone who uses mathematical or other technical skills to break into protected computer networks.

Handler In espionage, a spy who is responsible for collecting intelligence from other spies and transmitting it to the intelligence agency.

Intelligence Secret information including the information gained from the interception and decryption of coded messages.

Intelligence Agency An organisation devoted to the gathering of intelligence, such as the CIA.

Intercept To capture a communications signal intended for a different destination. In World War II, coded messages sent by radio were intercepted with a receiver.

Iron Curtain Phrase coined by British Prime minister, Winston Churchill to describe the division between democracies and communist states taking shape in Europe after 1946.

Magic Name given to the intelligence gained from intercepting and decrypting Japanese Purple messages in World War II.

Microfilm Photographic film containing images that are reduced in size. Used for photographing documents.

Misinformation False information designed to mislead a rival or enemy.

Morse Code A system of dots and dashes to represent the letters of the alphabet, transmitted by telegraph.

Nazis A political party which rose to power on the promise that it would make Germany mighty again after its humiliating defeat in World War I and which, under the leadership of Adolph Hitler, started World War II in an effort to dominate the rest of the world.

Neutral In wartime this means taking no side. Switzerland was a neutral country in World War II.

Open source intelligence Information from publicly available sources that is of interest to spies.

Plaintext Ordinary text that has been decrypted or is about to be encrypted.

Purple Name given to the cipher machine used by Japanese diplomats to encrypt their messages in World War II.

Ration card A card that gave the bearer the right to buy rationed goods. In many places in World War II, most food was rationed, or distributed in limited supplies.

Resistance A secret group or groups working towards the overthrow of forces occupying or invading their homeland.

Sabotage Destruction of equipment to weaken an enemy.

Superpower A nation that is superior in political and military power. During the Cold War, the United States and Soviet Union were the world's superpowers.

Surveillance Observing or monitoring someone secretly, often with the use of electronic equipment such as telephone taps.

Undercover Using an assumed identity. Spies usually operate undercover.

Ultra Name given to the intelligence gained from intercepting and decrypting German Enigma messages in World War II

Vet A check on someone's history. Potential spies are often vetted by intelligence agencies.

Walk-in A walk-in spy is one who volunteers his or her services to an intelligence agency, rather than one who is recruited by that agency.

INDEX

A

Abwehr 13, 19, 41, 42, 43
Afghanistan 29
al-Qaeda 39
Allies 8, 9, 10, 11, 12, 16, 19, 31, 33, 41
Ames, Aldrich 28-29, 30
Atlantic, Battle of the 19
Atomic
  secrets 26
  warfare 21, 37
Axis 8, 10, 21, 24

B

Bentley, Elizabeth 43
Berlin Wall 25, 27, 30, 31
Bletchley Park 11, 16, 17, 19, 20, 33, 40
Blunt, Anthony 25, 42
Bombe 11, 18-19, 40
Bond, James 10, 23, 32, 33, 34, 37, 41
Bourne Identity, The (film) 7, 34
Burgess, Guy 25, 26, 42

C

Cambridge Five 24, 25, 34
Camp X 9, 17
Canaris, Wilhelm 13, 41
Child, Julia 37
Churchill, Winston 8, 11
CIA 7, 10, 11, 12, 28, 30, 34, 40, 42, 43
Cipher machine 6, 8, 17, 18, 19, 20, 21, 22, 40
Cold War 4, 5, 6, 24-31, 32,

33, 34, 35, 36
Connery, Sean 32
Cornioley, Pearl 41
Cruise, Tom 34
Cryptanalysts 17, 20
Cuban Missile Crisis 25, 27

D

Damon, Matt 7, 34
Declaration of War 11, 14, 15
Defection 26, 27, 28, 29, 36, 42
Double agents 8, 10, 12, 13, 19, 25, 28, 29, 33, 42, 43
Dulles, Allen 10-11, 42

E

Economic Espionage 38-39
Enigma (film) 17, 33
Enigma Machine 9, 11, 13, 16, 17, 18, 19, 20, 22, 40, 42

F

Faulks, Sebastian 37
FBI 4, 9, 13, 26, 28, 29, 31, 33, 36, 43
Fleming, Ian 33, 34. 37, 41
Friedman, Elizebeth 20
Friedman, William 9, 13, 20, 21, 22, 40

G

Government Communications
  Headquarters (GCHQ) 16
Great Depression 24
Greene, Graham 33
Grotjan, Genevieve 20

GRU 29, 43

H

Hackers 7, 39
Hall, Virginia 40
Hanssen, Robert 30, 36
Harris, Robert 33
Hayden, Sterling 37
Hiroshima 21
Hitler, Adolf 11, 12, 18, 21, 41
Hoover, J. Edgar 33
House on 92nd Street, The (film) 33

I

International Spy Museum 33, 35
Internet 7, 39
Iron Cross 13
Iwo Jima 19, 23

J

Johnston, Philip 22-23
Jolie, Angelina 35

K

KGB 6, 25, 27, 28, 29, 30, 31, 33, 35, 36, 38, 43
Kolbe, Fritz 10, 11, 12, 42
Korean War 23, 27
Kühn family 14-15

L

Le Carré, John 25, 27, 32, 33, 34
Litvinenko, Alexander 35, 37

M

Maclean, Donald 24, 25, 26, 27, 42

Magicians 19-21, 22

Marks, Leo 31

Masterman, Sir John Cecil 11

McKinnon, Gary 7

MI5 4, 11, 12, 13, 33, 39, 42

MI6 4, 43

Mission: Impossible (film) 7, 34, 35

Morse Code 9

Mossad 37-38, 39

Mr and Mrs Smith (film) 35

N

Nagasaki 21

Next of Kin, The (film) 32

Nixon, President Richard M. 6, 29

Noble, Johnny 14

North Atlantic Treaty Organisation (NATO) 23, 24

O

Office of Strategic Services (OSS) 9, 10-11, 35, 37

Operation Double Cross 11-13, 19

P

Pearl Harbor 14, 15, 17

Penkovsky, Oleg 43

Philby, Kim 25, 26, 27, 34, 42

Pitt, Brad 35

Polish Cipher Bureau 9

Polyakov, Dmitri 29-30

Primrose, Operation 13, 19

Propaganda 8, 32

Pujol, Juan 43

Purple Code 13, 19, 20, 21, 40

Putin, Vladimir 31

R

Rejewski, Marian 18

Roosevelt, President Franklin, D. (FDR) 8, 19

Rosenbergs 23, 26, 27, 43

S

Schmidt, Hans-Thilo 18

Schmidt, Wulf 12

Sebold, William 13, 33,

Shadow army 9, 32

war 8

Shayler, David 33

Sigaba 22, 40

Signals Intelligence Service (SIS) 9, 22

Special Operations Executive (SOE) 8, 9, 10, 11, 12, 16, 19, 31, 33, 41

Spy Kids (film) 35

Spy satellites 5, 7, 24

Spy Who Came in From the Cold, The (film) 27

Stalin, Joseph 8, 21, 26, 27

Sunday Times, The (newspaper) 37

T

Tretyakov, Sergei 36

Tupelov TU-144 38

Turing, Alan 11, 16, 18, 40

Twenty Committee 11

U

U-2 planes 31, 32

U-boats 13, 19

Ultra intelligence 17, 19, 42

V

Vanunu, Mordecai 29, 37-38, 39

Venona, Project 26

Vietnam War 27

W

Walker, John Anthony 27-28, 29

Warsaw Pact 24, 25

Watergate Hotel 6

Welbike 12

Whistleblower 31, 33, 36, 37

Windtalkers (film) 33, 35

World War II 4, 5, 6, 8, 10, 11, 16, 21, 22, 24, 25, 32, 33, 34, 35, 40, 41, 42, 43

Y

Yoshikawa, Takeo 15

V

Zedong, Chairman Mao 23, 29

ACKNOWLEDGMENTS

PICTURE CREDITS:

Every effort has been made to trace the copyright holders, and we apologise in advance for any unintentional omissions. We would be pleased to insert the appropriate acknowledgments in any subsequent edition of this publication.

B=bottom; C=centre; L=left; R=right; T=top

Stefano Archetti/Rex Features: 6t. beretta/sims/Rex Features: 4t. Bettmann/CORBIS: 26-27, 43tl. Buena Vista/RGA: 33t. CNN via Getty Images: 36b. Thomas Coex/AFP/Getty Images: 37b. CORBIS: 10-11, 15b, 23t, 42tl. Matt Crypto/Wikimedia Commons: 16b. Geoff Dann © Dorling Kindersley, Courtesy of the Imperial War Museum, London: 9t. Geoff Dann © Dorling Kindersley, Courtesy of Lorraine Electronics Surveillance: 6b. History is a Hoot, Inc. www.historyisahoot.com: 40tr. Hulton Archive/Getty Images: 8-9. BOB DAUGHERTY/AP/PA Photos: 28b. Lear21/Wikimedia Commons: 30t. Lewis Durham/Rex Features: 15t. Evening Standard/Getty Images: OFCt,OBC (background). Everett Collection/Rex Features: 17b. Jon Freeman/Rex Features: 22-23. Getty Images: 36t. Hodder & Stoughton. Used with permission: 34t. iStock: OBCtr, bl, br. Nils Jorgensen/Rex Features: 4-5c, 48. Keystone/Hulton Archive/Getty Images: 24b, 25b, 27b, 30-31. Keystone/Getty Images: 12t. Herbie Knott/Rex Features: 42b. Life Magazine/Life Magazine/Time & Life Pictures/Getty Images: 16t, 40tl. MGM/RGA: 35t. Darz Mol/ Wikimedia Commons: 29t. Harry Myers/Rex Features: 41tr. NASA: 38-39. National Archives, RG226: 10t. National Archives and Records Administration: 11c. Courtesy of the National Security Agency: 1, 19c, 20t, 20-21, 21t, 22t, 40b. Navy Historical Center: 14tr. Pictorial Press Ltd / Alamy: 20b. Popperfoto/Getty Images: 13b, 19r, 41tl, 42tr. Press Agency/Getty Images: 18t. Rex Features: 7b, 8t, 32b, 33b, 41b. Roger-Viollet/Rex Features: 13t. Mark Rucker/Transcendental Graphics, Getty Images: 11t. Dave Rudkin © Dorling Kindersley, Courtesy of the RAF Museum, Hendon: 5b. Dave Rudkin © Dorling Kindersley, Courtesy of the Royal Signals Museum, Blandford Camp, Dorset: 12b. Shutterstock: OBCtl, OFCb, 4-5(background), 5t, 6-7(background), 7t, 25t, 27t, 31t, 38t. Sipa Press/Rex Features: 4bl, 14tl, 24-25, 28t, 29b, 36-37, 39t. Stuzhin & Cheredintzev/Keystone/Hulton Archive/Getty Images: 43tr. Swim Ink 2, LLC/CORBIS: 32t. ticktock media archive: 24t. Cherie A. Thurlby/US Department of Defense: 31b. Universal/Everett/Rex Features: 6-7c. UPPA/Photoshot: 34b. Wikimedia Commons: 18b, 43b.